— ✳✳✳✳✳ —

J Golden Kimball's

GOLDEN MOMENTS

Arnold Dee White
Former Secretary to Elder J. Golden Kimball

— ✵✵✵✵✵ —

ISBN: 1-55517-164-8

925 North Main, Springville, UT 84663 • 801/489-4084

CFI
Cedar Fort, Incorporated
CFI Distribution • CFI Books • Inside Cougar Report
Tapestry Press • Health & Wellness Report

Cover Design by Lyle Mortimer
Page Layout and Design by Lyle Mortimer
Printed in the United States of America

Introduction

J. Golden Kimball was in his early or middle eighties at the time of my appointment as his secretary. Because of his physical condition, he relied on me somewhat for minor things that did not involve the council. So I had a rather intimate relationship with Brother Kimball.

I loved and admired him, had unbounded confidence in his integrity and devotion to the work of God. I always found him to be a true friend and brother. And I think I can honestly say that anyone that really knew Brother Kimball and knew his heart couldn't help but love him.

— ✳✳✳✳✳ —

At the early age of twenty-two he moved with his mother, then a widow, and her other children into Rich County, and in that cold outpost set to work to further extend the settlement of that community. In his youth and young manhood he was first a teamster; next, a rancher and cattle-raiser; then a merchant. Finally, he was called to the pursuits that are his heritage by birth and character—a guide and teacher in the enrichment of life. He performed valiant service as a missionary for the church through years when his body was racked with fever. In 1892, he was called to the First Council of the Seventy.

Brother Golden, as we affectionately know him, was a true product of the West, with humor as

— ✻✻✻✻✻ —

dry as our desert sands but as refreshing as our canyon breezes, with a philosophy as beautiful as our twilights and as brilliant as our noon-day sun. He has endeared himself to us for the high quality of his mind, his patience, and straightforwardness.

Arnold Dee White

Golden Moments

— ❋❋❋❋❋ —

— ✳✳✳✳✳ —

One of the Brethren one time said, "Brother Kimball, why do you use so many 'damns' and 'hells' in your sermons?"

"Well, if I didn't use a good hard damn once in a while they wouldn't pay any more attention to what I say than they do to what you say."

— ✻✻✻✻✻ —

Brother Kimball enjoyed the gift of healing. During the years that I was in the office of the First Council, whenever it was known that President Kimball was at the office, there would be a train of people constantly coming in to receive blessings.

— ✳✳✳✳✳ —

One particular day, about thirteen people had called on J. Golden Kimball for blessings with which I helped him. He was in his eighty-fifth or eighty-sixth year, and the energy and strength it took to administer to all of these people just about knocked him out.

I think it was along about nearly five-o'clock when we finished the thirteenth administration. As the door closed behind, J. Golden Kimball slumped back on the big council table and said: "Brother White, I can't understand why so many people come to me to be blessed for their health when I'm near damn dead myself."

— ✳✳✳✳✳ —

I remember attending general conference with Mother and Father. The seats we had were in the high balcony of the far east side of the Tabernacle. As a little boy I had a faint recollection of President Joseph F. Smith. He called on President Kimball to speak. I don't remember any of the other speakers at the conference, but I do remember one thing that President Kimball said:

— ✳✳✳✳✳ —

"A man can do about everything that's wrong and evil and cussed in his life, and then you go to his funeral and you hear some of the sweetest, loveliest, nicest things said about him that aren't necessarily right. If they did that at my funeral, I'd kick the hell out of the coffin."

— ✳✳✳✳✳ —

President Joseph F. Smith apparently had taken some exception to J. Golden Kimball's expressions and approach. I think it was Francis M. Lyman who was the President of the Quorum of the Twelve at that time, and Heber J. Grant was the next senior member. They were appointed as a committee to work on Brother Kimball to see if they couldn't tone him down a little bit. Apparently in the process they must have been a little severe with Brother Kimball.

I guess as elderly people sometimes do, J. Golden Kimball reflected on the past. He was making some observations one day about being taken to task, and he related this experience to me:

— ❋❋❋❋❋ —

"Brother White, they really got after me and they indicated that the approach I took wasn't a very intelligent thing to do. But as I started up that hill to home," he lived up on First North, "the farther I walked the madder I got, till I didn't give a damn if there was such a thing as intelligence."

"I brooded over that counsel all night long and it made me feel bad to think that I would be dealt with so vigorously. The next morning I was starting up the Church Office Building steps and Brother Lyman was coming out and apparently he sensed that they had been a little severe with me too, because he put his arm around me and slapped me on the shoulder and said, 'Brother Kimball, do you love

— ✳✳✳✳✳ —

your brethren?' I straightened up and looked him in
the eye and I said, 'Yes, but there's some I love a
damn site more that I do others.'"

— ✳✳✳✳✳ —

J. Golden Kimball was out somewhere with President B.H. Robert's, whom he succeeded in the Council. Brother Roberts, in his vigorous way, was transacting the business of the evening, I think unconsciously in some minor disregard of Brother Kimball's being present. After Brother Robert's had gone ahead and accomplished most of the business of the evening, he apparently sensed that Brother Kimball was there and that maybe he should have something to say as the evening had worn on. So he said to Brother Kimball:

— ✳✳✳✳✳ —

"Brother Kimball, do you have anything to add to what I have said?"

"Only this, Brother Roberts—When you're gone I'll be the senior."

— ❋❋❋❋❋ —

In the midst of one of his prayers, he burst out in a loud laugh and said: "O Lord, forgive me; it makes me laugh to pray about some men."

— ✳✳✳✳✳ —

On the subject of money, J. Golden Kimball once said: "If I had a million dollars, I'd be the most sought after man in the Church. But I haven't got it—damn it."

— ✳✳✳✳✳ —

Walking into a clothing store, J. Golden Kimball approached a clerk and said: "I'd like to see a suit that will fit me."

The clerk, eying the tall, skinny figure of his prospect replied, "Hell, so would I."

— ✳✳✳✳✳ —

About the brethren: "Brother White, I'd like to get mad at the Brethren once and a while, but dammit, if I did I'd blow a fuse. The doctor told me I've got to shut up and keep quiet, but it is the hardest thing I have to do."

— ❉❉❉❉❉ —

Antoine R. Irvins had been sent by the council to one of the stakes down toward the middle or central part of the state to see if they couldn't engender a little more life into one of the stake missions. Upon returning, he made his report of the visit and, among other things, indicated that we had a very competent, capable mission president down there. But, the mission president was experiencing some problems due to the fact that his wife wasn't too sympathetic about the amount of time that the missionary labors were requiring of her husband.

The only remark that Brother Kimball made after Brother Irvins made his report was this:

— ❋❋❋❋❋ —

"I'll wear the pants in my house even if they are out at the seat."

— ✳✳✳✳✳ —

As J. Golden Kimball was going North on the train, an old farmer got on the train in Bountiful; recognizing Brother Kimball, he took a seat beside him. The old farmer was hard of hearing, and like many deaf people, he spoke much louder than an ordinary person would.

— ✳✳✳✳✳ —

Brother Kimball asked the gentlemen if he was paying his tithing. He responded by saying: "Yes, but maybe not the way you would like me to; when I harvest my potatoes, I take the sack to certain widows; when I harvest my fruit, I share some of the crop with them. By sharing part of my harvest, I get a great deal of satisfaction. What do you think of that, Brother Kimball?" J Golden replied:

— ✳✳✳✳✳ —

"It appears to me that you're having a hell of a good time spending the Lord's money."

— ✻✻✻✻✻ —

One hot summer day, Brother Kimball and one of the Twelve Apostles were assigned to encourage the people to subscribe to the Improvement Era. After others had made their appeals, and the meeting was dragging on, Brother Kimball was called upon to speak. He stood at the pulpit and said:

— ✳✳✳✳✳ —

"It's a hell of a hot day, and many of you are tired out. How many of you will subscribe to the Era if I quit right now and let you go home?"

Needless to say, they took a record number of subscriptions that day.

— ✳✳✳✳✳ —

A certain bishop was having problems in his ward retiring the debt on the chapel. He asked J. Golden Kimball to come down and talk to the ward about it. J. Golden said he would come and bring a special musical number with him. The quartet was instructed not to sing one note on key. As the quartet was to sing a second number, he instructed them to sing better than they ever had before. After a most harmonious and beautiful rendition, he said:

— ✸✸✸✸✸ —

"Brothers and Sisters, you have a debt on your building, but you haven't been united enough to retire it. The quartet preached my sermon. The Lord bless you!"

— ✳✳✳✳✳ —

About his experiences, J. Golden Kimball remarked:

"I would not give my experience and the association I have had with the brethren or the authorities for all the riches in the world."

— ✳✳✳✳✳ —

God:

"I may not have a perfect and true conception of God, but I love God; I love him for his perfection; I love him for his mercy; I love him for his justice; and notwithstanding my many weaknesses I am not afraid to meet him. For I know that he will deal justly with me; and the great joy I have is that he will understand me."

— ✳✳✳✳✳ —

Scriptures:

"I don't believe the man lives, unless God inspires him, who can breathe into a book what you can get out of the Bible, Book of Mormon, Doctrine and Covenants and Pearl of Great Price. That is my testimony."

— ❋❋❋❋❋ —

Honesty:

"The Lord can do very little for a man who persists in being dishonest and untruthful. And, of course, it goes without saying that no man or woman in the Church of Jesus Christ can be immoral and have the Spirit of God to be with them."

— ✳✳✳✳✳ —

Responsibilites:

"I place my trust in God, the eternal Father, and it is my business to get a clear and true conception of God, and of Jesus Christ, and to realize that these men whom we have sustained are servants of the people. They are servants of God, and we sustain them, and we uphold them."

— ✳✳✳✳✳ —

Healing:

"I have got the gift to heal others. I have seen wonderful healings. Few men have seen more, unless they were better men. I have witnessed all kinds of diseases healed, but I could not get the faith to be healed. I failed. I just had enough faith to keep alive—that is all."

— ✳✳✳✳✳ —

Inspiration:

Under the influence of the Holy Ghost men are entitled to inspiration, to revelation, to dreams and visions, for their own salvation. But that is as far as you can go. And any person who thinks he is living so close to God that he can direct this Church, unless he repents he will apostatize, as surely as God lives. God never gave us inspiration and revelation to take the place of the Prophet of the living God.

— ✳✳✳✳✳ —

About the Bible:

I would advise myself and every other man and woman in this Church to read the Bible. It is not read as much as it should be. The same is true of the Book of Mormon, Doctrine and Covenants and Pearl of Great Price. You will find within the lids of those great books many prophecies and revelations. And if you will go to God and ask him in humility if these things are true he will give you the testimony, and you will know.

— ✻✻✻✻✻ —

Testimony:

My testimony, brethren and sisters, in all confidence, is that I know this work is true. I have tested it out. I have found God. I am a man of weakness; I am a man full of faults; but God knows I have given him the best effort there was in me.

— ✳✳✳✳✳ —

About conference:

My brethren and sisters, I have been hanging on the hook so long during this conference that I am nearly exhausted. I have had some wonderful thoughts, but have waited so long they have nearly all oozed out of me.

— ❋❋❋❋❋ —

Filling the niche:

How much good we do, no man knoweth. I claim that every man fills his niche when he is called of God and set apart and ordained to an office. He may not fill it in the way someone else would fill it, but if he is a man of courage he will fill it in his own way, under the influence of the Holy Spirit.

— ✳✳✳✳✳ —

Judgment:

"Well, but do you think that by and by when you go up there, he will pass you right off or stop you and ask a few questions?"

"Being skinny, I may squeeze by. I think, however, he may want me to clear up a few things."

— ✳✳✳✳✳ —

Bankers:

As is well known, bankers were not in very good repute during the depression, and on one occasion one of them jocularly accosted J. Golden Kimball and said: "Brother Kimball, you shouldn't use such language as you employ in our church gatherings."

To which Golden retorted, "I don't think this is a time for bankers to be giving advice to anybody."

— ✳✳✳✳✳ —

Truth:

I want to tell you in a few words that there is
nothing in the world that the wicked dislike so much
as the truth.

— ✻✻✻✻✻ —

Growing old:

Everywhere I go among this people they look at me with sympathy and pity, and ask my how my health is. Only a few days ago I walked down Main Street three blocks, and twelve people asked me that question. And I felt like kicking the last one.

— ✳✳✳✳✳ —

Debt:

I can tell you how to keep out of debt; but I can't tell you how to get out after you get in.

— ❄❄❄❄❄ —

Shaking hands:

I have shaken hands with some men when I would just as soon have put my hands into a bucket of ice water as to shake hands with them. They may have been friendly, but had no means of showing their feelings. Great sermons have been preached in this Church by the simple shaking of hands.

— ✳✳✳✳✳ —

Thankfulness:

I feel sometimes like the little freckle-faced, red-headed boy who was asked by his teacher, in Sunday School, to tell how thankful he was to the Lord: "Teacher, I don't know what to be thankful for; God purty nigh ruined me."

— ❋❋❋❋❋ —

Charity:

As long as a man has a righteous object he has a right to make an effort, and if he makes any mistakes, it is my duty to reach out to him my hand, even the hand of charity.

— ❋❋❋❋❋ —

Compassion:

Brethren and Sisters, we can afford to be sympathetic; we can afford of all people on the earth to be filled with sympathy and compassion. I am not concerned very much about what other religionists do. I am not concerned about the Christian Scientists; I have little to say against them. If they do any good that is their business, but no church or lodge can find a more successful way of making inroads among our people than by getting them to extend the hand of sympathy, love and affection in their trials and tribulations.

— ✳✳✳✳✳ —

Repentance:

What can God do for a liar who refuses to
repent? Can the Lord save him? He can't claim
salvation. Baptizing him in water will not settle the
trouble, unless you keep him under.

— ✳✳✳✳✳ —

Securing hearts:

The Lord can accomplish great things, but he wants the people, and he will never be satisfied until he secures the hearts of the children of men.

— ✳✳✳✳✳ —

Eternal Life:

The greatest of all gifts is eternal life, but we
have to pay for it, just like our fathers and mothers
did. We will have to pay for it with service, and with
sacrifice, as there can be no blessings obtained
without sacrifice. I know what is the matter. We
think more of automobiles, we think more of
oriental-rugs and hundred-dollar gowns than we do
of salvation.

— ✳✳✳✳✳ —

Suffering:

My brethren and sisters, the short time I occupy I want to say to you that my knowledge is very limited, and it does not take me very long to tell it; but what I do know, I know as well as any man in this Church from the least to the greatest. Why do I know it? Because I have learned it through the things which I have suffered. We have to suffer sometimes, before we are meek and humble and have faith in God.

— ✳✳✳✳✳ —

Death:

      Why fear death? That is what I am talking about to myself all the time. People have been looking for it in my case for a considerable length of time, but I have fooled them up to date; and I am trying to learn not to fear death.

— ✳✳✳✳✳ —

The Lord's side:

"I hope that the Lord is on our side." That is what all these nations are hoping, that the Lord is on their side. And President Lincoln said, "Well, I am not much concerned about the Lord being on our side," which was quite a shock to the ministers. "I am not concerned about that. What I am most concerned about is whether we are on the Lord's side." That is what I want you to be concerned about.

— ❋❋❋❋❋ —

Callings:

I haven't been called, nor asked to do anything, that I have not responded to. No appointment has been given me that I have not filled, in my way, and to the best of my ability.

I can do anything I am set apart to do, if I have the spirit of my appointment and am humble and prayerful.

— ❊❊❊❊❊ —

God's gift:

Of all the gifts and all the blessings that God can give to his children, the "greatest gift is salvation."

— ❊❊❊❊❊ —

Land of liberty:

I am proud of the fact that I am a natural born heir, and was given birth in this land of liberty and freedom. We are not called upon to cry out, "All hail to the king."

— ❊❊❊❊❊ —

Church membership:

I thank God I belong to a church which is the Church of Jesus Christ of Latter-day Saints. It does not belong to President Joseph F. Smith, and he made no such claim, but it belongs to God the Father and to his son, Jesus Christ.

— ✻✻✻✻✻ —

Sickness:

I have been trying to be sick for a couple of years, and I have rather fizzled out at it. I feel a good deal like the story I read the other day. "Some fellow was sitting on the pier that reached out into the ocean—and he fell in, and he hollered, 'Help! help! I can't swim.' And an old fellow was sitting on the pier fishing, and he said: 'Neither can I, but I wouldn't brag.'"

— ❀❀❀❀❀ —

Presiding:

I was with an apostle on a trip in the South and we found a Bishop without any people. He wept, and came to the apostle to know what to do. "Well, you will have to stay here until some people come to you." All the people he had was his wife— and anybody that can preside over his wife, I take my hat off to him.

— ❋❋❋❋❋ —

Prayer:

I have a prayer that I offer sometimes when I walk by the wayside, and I say: "I now place myself and all my affairs" —I haven't got any affairs, however— "in the kind care and keeping of the Father, with a loving trust, knowing that all things are working for my best good."

— ❋❋❋❋❋ —

Faith:

"The Lord is my shepherd." Do you believe that? "The Lord is my shepherd; I shall not want." Then why worry your head off for fear you will go to the poor house?

— ✻✻✻✻✻ —

Fear:

Do not let doubt and fear creep into your hearts, for God never planted in one of his children the spirit of fear; it does not come from God. For when you have faith in God, you have no fear, you have no doubt; you know. But you will have trials and be tested; you will eat the bread of adversity and drink the water of affliction. That is the only thing that will keep you humble.

— ✳✳✳✳✳ —

Agency:

"I have my agency and individuality, but
when I joined the Church, I waived the right to sin."

— ✻✻✻✻✻ —

Priesthood:

One stormy winter day, as Brother Kimball started out to cross the street, an inconsiderate motorist splashed hum with slushy, muddy water. Brother Kimball, stepping back and regaining his composure, said: "That man doesn't show any respect for the Priesthood."

— ✳✳✳✳✳ —

Marriage:

One day at the pulpit, Brother Kimball said, "Brethren, there isn't one man in a thousand who knows how to treat his wife." As all the sisters nudged their husbands, he then said:

"Sisters, there isn't one woman in ten thousand who knows when she is well treated."

— ✳✳✳✳✳ —

Forgiveness:

Now, brethren, let us repent if we have got any bitterness in our hearts toward each other--let us be generous, and forgiving. No man has any influence or power for good when angry.

— ✻✻✻✻✻ —

About the Spirit:

I never was afraid of a mob in the Southern states when I had the Spirit of God, but I was scared pretty nearly to death after the Spirit left.

— ❋❋❋❋❋ —

Religion:

A man who considers his religion a slavery has not begun to comprehend the real nature of religion.

— ✳✳✳✳✳ —

Spiritual awareness:

I say to you, as a servant of the Lord and as a watchman upon the towers, it's high time that we are looking up. I tell you, if there is anything on earth that we need in the Church, in this day in which we live, it is not money or temporal power, but it is a spiritual uplifiting, and it must be taking place in Zion, or else there will be a falling away.

— ✳✳✳✳✳ —

Parentage:

I am very proud of my parentage. I do not think any one appreciates his parentage more than I do. But, I want to say to the Latter-day Saints that pride in parentage won't save you. If we get salvation, we must keep the commandments, and serve the Lord.

— ❋❋❋❋❋ —

Half-way men:

There is a class of men, I call them half-way men; I pray to God I may never be found among them. I would rather be dead than to be numbered among half-way men, persons who have plaster-cast expressions on their faces and are without hearts, without souls, wihtout love and bigness.

— ❋❋❋❋❋ —

Criticism:

Because of your severe criticisms and your unkind statements, God will hold you responsible.

— ❋❋❋❋❋ —

Sacrifice:

"Brethren," the shrill voice began, "how many of you would give your lives for this Church?" Every hand went up.

"How many of you would give fifty cents to the seventies' fund?"

— ❋❋❋❋❋ —

Equality:

     I love God for one thing, if nothing else: That He gives to every one of His children, black or white, bond or free, an equal chance.

— ✳✳✳✳✳ —

The Spirit of God:

I have learned that the Spirit of God gives you joy and peace and patience and long-suffering and gentleness, and you have the spirit of forgiveness and you love the souls of the children of men.

— ✳✳✳✳✳ —

Serving a mission:

I will go on a mission if called. I am not just talking either, God knows it, and I know it. I would go if I were brought back in a casket.

— ❋❋❋❋❋ —

Faith in the Church:

I would rather be tied to a whipping post and have my flesh stripped from my bones than to lose my faith in this Church and have my spirit killed.

— ❋❋❋❋❋ —

Helping others:

As long as a man has a righteous object he
has a right to make an effort, and if he makes any
mistakes, it is my duty to reach out to him my hand,
even the hand of charity.

— ✽✽✽✽✽ —

Enduring:

Now I grant, my brethren and sisters, that sometimes we have to endure many things, and I presume that if we live the Gospel of the Lord Jesus Christ we shall have to endure all things; but it requires a very prayerful heart to enable us to endure some things.

— ✻✻✻✻✻ —

Exercising faith:

The Lord's ways are not as man's ways, and He does things so differently from the way we want to do them that many of us are oftentimes surprised, and it requires constant faith to stay in this Church. I believe it is the hardest church to stay in that there is on earth, because you have always got to keep exercising faith. I remember hearing of a man that apostatized from the Church, and he was asked what was the matter. He said, "Well, I have got tired exercising faith."

— ✳✳✳✳✳ —

The organization of the Church:

Some find a great deal of fault with the Church. I want to tell you there is no fault in the organization of the Church; it is perfect. There is no fault in the Gospel of Christ; if lived up to, it makes you better; it makes you good in your home; it makes you good to your wife, and good to your children. It makes you good on the streets; it makes you honest; it makes you kind and generous. I know that-- nobody knows it better than I do. That is what the relgion of Christ does.

— ✳✳✳✳✳ —

Self-righteousness:

We need not pull long faces and put on an air of self-righteousness, thinking it indicates faith and is more pleasing to the Lord.

— ✸✸✸✸✸ —

Salvation:

I am very doubtful if a man can be saved in the Kingdom of God who has no individuality, and does not assert his agency, because salvation is an individual work.

— ✳✳✳✳✳ —

Tests:

Every man in this Church will be tested to the core; they will be proved as Abraham was proved, and when the Lord is satisfied that they love Him and will keep His commandments, then He will come to their rescue.

— ❋❋❋❋❋ —

Trying:

     Any man who tries to do the right thing and continues to try, is not a failure in the sight of the Lord.

— ❋❋❋❋❋ —

The Spirit of repentance:

A man can't repent simply because an apostle tells him to repent; he can't do it until he gets the spirit of repentance, which is a gift from God; and some of us don't get it very quickly.

— ✳✳✳✳✳ —

Seeing things right:

      Some of us don't get the spirit of repentance
and see things right until our hair is gray.

— ❋❋❋❋❋ —

Doing wrong:

You never saw a man in your life do a wrong thing who was happy over it.

— ✳✳✳✳✳ —

Tolerance:

Let us be tolerant.

— ✻✻✻✻✻ —

Kindness:

Let us be kind and considerate.

— ❈❈❈❈❈ —

Charity:

It is the proper thing to despise sin and
wickedness; but I think it is wrong to despise the
man that has a weakness and make him feel that he is
good for nothing.

— ✳✳✳✳✳ —

Truth:

Every Latter-day Saint in the Church should receive every truth, or else none of it.

— ❄❄❄❄❄ —

Supporting missionaries:

If you can't go on missions; if you are too rich to go, or you have too much business, or you have positions in the Church that prevent you from going; then, for heaven's sake, help those who do go.

— ❋❋❋❋❋ —

Borrowed light:

    Latter-day Saints, you must think for yourselves. No man or woman can remain in this Church on borrowed light.

— ❋❋❋❋❋ —

Members:

If the Church could have been destroyed,
some, who claim to be members in the Church,
would have destroyed it years ago.

— ✳✳✳✳✳ —

The Church:

    I don't care how much harm is committed by pretended members of this Church, they can't destroy it; they will destroy themselves.

— ❈❈❈❈❈ —

Covenants:

If you want to stay with this Church, be true to your covenants.

— ✳✳✳✳✳ —

Fault-finding:

If you can handle your own home and mind your own business, you will have no time for fault-finding.

— ✳✳✳✳✳ —

Prejudice:

   The most dangerous thing that menaces us is to get prejudiced. How I hate it!

— ✻✻✻✻✻ —

Justness:

No man that lives in the flesh can be prejudiced and be just.

— ❋❋❋❋❋ —

Writing:

I write books, but I put them in pigeon holes and lock them up where they cannot do any damage.

— ❋❋❋❋❋ —

Goodness:

I have heard so much about goodness that sometimes I get unhappy, even at conference, and I feel like a little girl I heard of that did wrong. Her mother importuned her and labored with her, just as we have labored with you people, and she said, "Mother, don't try to make me good; shoot me."

— ✻✻✻✻✻ —

Choosing a wife:

Some select a girl because she has pretty eyes; some because she has pretty hair. I knew a man who chose a girl because she could sing. He married her, and the next morning, when he saw her without any paint or powder on, and saw a part of her hair on the dresser, he looked at her and said, "Sing, for hell sakes, sing!"

— ❊❊❊❊❊ —

Callings:

It is marvelous in my sight how men that are called by divine authority increase in wisdom and knowledge, how they progress, and how well they fill their positions when they have the spirit of their office and calling.

— ❋❋❋❋❋ —

Advice for missionaries:

    Missionaries, don't allow any woman to take your arm. Keep them at arm's length.

— ✻✻✻✻✻ —

Zion:

I want to say you, my brethren and sisters,
that all is not well in Zion.

— ✻✻✻✻✻ —

Sin:

The great sin that is creeping in among this people, together with other wordly sins, is the sin of adultery.

— ❋❋❋❋❋ —

Positions:

Some of you place too much stress upon the
positions that men hold in the Church.

— ✳✳✳✳✳ —

Blessings:

You do not have to be apostles, you do not have to be presidents of stakes, nor bishops to enjoy the gifts and blessings pertaining to the Gospel of the Lord, Jesus Christ.

— ❋❋❋❋❋ —

Duty:

There is danger in exalted position, and where "much is given much is required."

— ✹✹✹✹✹ —

The world:

This world was not made just to hold people imbued with selfishness and unhappiness, with no ambition beyond eating, drinking, and begetting.

— ❋❋❋❋❋ —

Purpose:

We ought to plan ahead, have some purpose.

— ✳✳✳✳✳ —

Opportunity:

Life means opportunity.

— ✳✳✳✳✳ —

Development:

Life means development.

— ❋❋❋❋❋ —

Life:

Life well spent means knowledge, growth, simplicity of life, and complexity of thought .

— ✳✳✳✳✳ —

The body of the church:

When I look over this body of men, I do not discover that you are very distinguished in appearance. Why, you are no better looking than I am, and I look pretty bad.

— ✻✻✻✻✻ —

The youth:

I can see only one course of safety for the young people of this Church, and that is to teach them they should have an abiding faith in God the Father, in His Son, Jesus Christ, and in the Holy Ghost.

— ❋❋❋❋❋ —

About the dead:

    I would like to preach a man's funeral
sermon while he is living; you can't tell the truth
about him when he is dead. "

— ✻✻✻✻✻ —

Good-naturedness:

I do think it's best to get the people good-natured and in a mood to take what you give them. You remember what my father used to say about giving the baby medicine. "Just tickle it under the chin and down goes the medicine." That's always seemed better to me than the old-fashioned method of using force or too much persuasion.

— ❈❈❈❈❈ —

About himself:

     I know my way is different, but I can't help that. It seems I was made that way.

— ✳✳✳✳✳ —

Language:

What about those two little words that seem, now and again, to worry the authorities? Oh, I never intend to use them when I get up to speak, but they just come to me as naturally as singing to a bird.

— ✳✳✳✳✳ —

Change:

Do you think you ought to ask a leopard to change his spots this late in life?

— ❋❋❋❋❋ —

Religion:

Well, religion to my mind means more than to be pious and prayerful. You need these things if you can get them. But the bigger things are to love your God, your neighbor, to be generous to the poor, to be honest, truthful, moral, etc., to repent, to sell all you have, leave your family, home, country and follow the Master. These things to me are evidence of faith in God.

— ❋❋❋❋❋ —

Sentiments from J. Golden Kimball, written down with a desire that they be read at the time of his funeral services.

— ✳✳✳✳✳ —

I am indeed proud in saying, I am a soldier of
the Cross, a special witness for the Lord, being
clothed upon with the spirit of my appointment and
having a desire and being prepared to go to the
front—when called—and be one of the soldiers of
the firing lines.

— ✹✹✹✹✹ —

About the Author

Arnold Dee White worked as secretary to the Quorum of the Seventy during the last two years of President J. Golden Kimball's life. During that time President Kimball was the senior president. Brother White continued to work as secretary to the quorum until 1946 when he was drafted by the Melchizedek Priesthood Committee as secretary.

He later worked in real estate and building. He retired in 1975 when he and his wife were called on a mission to Hawaii. They later served missions in Richmond, Virginia, San Diego, California, and in the Tempe, AZ mission.

— ✳✳✳✳✳ —

As a young man Brother White served a full-time mission in England. He married Erma Manwill in 1934. They have three children, 24 grandchildren, 26 greatgranchildren, "and more to come."

Golden Moments

— ✳✳✳✳✳ —

Bibliography
J. Golden Kimball by Claude Richards
The Story of a unique personality.
copyright 1934 by Claude Richards